Murray

To:

From:

D1738698

The Messiah

THE STORY OF THE NATIVITY

THE GOSPEL ACCORDING
TO ST. LUKE, CHAPTER 2, KJV

PETER PAUPER PRESS
White Plains, New York

p. 6: © Geoffrey Clements/Corbis
p. 10: © National Gallery Collection; By kind permission of the
Trustees of the National Gallery, London/Corbis
p. 16: © Archivo Iconografico, S.A./Corbis
p. 19: © Arte & Immagini srl/Corbis
p. 24: © Arte & Immagini srl/Corbis
p. 29: © Arte & Immagini srl/Corbis
p. 35: © North Carolina Museum of Art/Corbis
p. 38: © Francis G. Mayer/Corbis
p. 45: © Christie's Images/Corbis
p. 52: © Philadelphia Museum of Art/Corbis

Copyright © 2002
Peter Pauper Press, Inc.
202 Mamaroneck Avenue
White Plains, NY 10601
All rights reserved
ISBN 0-88088-418-5
Printed in China
7 6 5 4 3 2 1

Visit us at www.peterpauper.com

The Messiah

The Story of the Nativity

Introduction

❖

Over two thousand years ago a star rose above Bethlehem heralding the birth of Jesus, the Light of the World. The Gospel of Luke recounts this wondrous story, beginning with Mary and Joseph's journey from Nazareth to Bethlehem, where Christ was born in a manger, as there was no room at the inn. An angel proclaimed the joyful event to shepherds, who followed the brightest star to the babe and bowed down before him.

Luke's Gospel presents Jesus as a serene, strong, and ethical teacher. The Nativity tells the story through Christ's twelfth year, when he fulfilled the prophccy:

"Fear not: for behold, I bring you good tidings of great joy, which shall be to all people."

And it came to pass in those days, that there went out a decree from Caesar Augustus, that all the world should be taxed.

(And this taxing was first made when Cyrenius was governor of Syria.)

And all went to be taxed, every one into his own city.

And Joseph also went up
from Galilee, out of the city
of Nazareth, into Judaea,
unto the city of David,
which is called Bethlehem;
(because he was of the house
and lineage of David:)

To be taxed with Mary
his espoused wife,
being great with child.

And so it was, that, while they were there, the days were accomplished that she should be delivered.

And she brought forth her
firstborn son, and wrapped
him in swaddling clothes,
and laid him in a manger;
because there was no room
for them in the inn.

And there were in the same country shepherds abiding in the field, keeping watch over their flock by night.

And, lo, the angel of the Lord
came upon them, and the
glory of the Lord shone
round about them:
and they were sore afraid.

And the angel said unto them,
Fear not: for, behold, I bring
you good tidings of great joy,
which shall be to all people.

For unto you is born this day
in the city of David a Saviour,
which is Christ the Lord.

And this shall be a
sign unto you;
Ye shall find the babe
wrapped in swaddling clothes,
lying in a manger.

And suddenly there was
with the angel a multitude
of the heavenly host
praising God, and saying,

Glory to God in the highest,
and on earth peace,
good will toward men.

And it came to pass, as the angels were gone away from them into heaven, the shepherds said one to another, Let us now go even unto Bethlehem, and see this thing which is come to pass, which the Lord hath made known unto us.

And they came with haste,
and found Mary, and Joseph,
and the babe lying in a manger.

And when they had seen it,
they made known abroad
the saying which was told
them concerning this child.

And all they that heard it
wondered at those things
which were told them by
the shepherds.

But Mary kept all these things,
and pondered them in her heart.

And the shepherds returned,
glorifying and praising
God for all the things that
they had heard and seen,
as it was told unto them.

And when eight days were
accomplished for the circumcising
of the child, his name was called
Jesus, which was so named
of the angel before he was
conceived in the womb.

And when the days of her
purification according to the law
of Moses were accomplished,
they brought him to Jerusalem,
to present him to the Lord;

(As it is written in the law of
the Lord, Every male that
openeth the womb shall be
called holy to the Lord;)

And to offer a sacrifice
according to that which is
said in the law of the Lord,
A pair of turtledoves,
or two young pigeons.

And, behold, there was a
man in Jerusalem, whose name
was Simeon; and the same
man was just and devout,
waiting for the consolation of
Israel: and the Holy Ghost
was upon him.

And it was revealed unto him
by the Holy Ghost, that he
should not see death, before
he had seen the Lord's Christ.

And he came by the Spirit
into the temple: and when the
parents brought in the child Jesus,
to do for him after the
custom of the law,

Then took he him up in his arms,
and blessed God, and said,

Lord, now lettest thou thy
servant depart in peace,
according to thy word:

For mine eyes have seen
thy salvation,

Which thou hast prepared
before the face of all people;

A light to lighten the Gentiles,
and the glory of thy people Israel.

And Joseph and his mother
marvelled at those things
which were spoken of him.

And Simeon blessed them,
and said unto Mary his mother,
Behold, this child is set for the
fall and rising again of many in
Israel; and for a sign which
shall be spoken against;

(Yea, a sword shall pierce
through thy own soul also,) that
the thoughts of many hearts
may be revealed.

And there was one Anna,
a prophetess, the daughter
of Phanuel, of the tribe of Aser:
she was of a great age, and had
lived with an husband seven
years from her virginity;

And she was a widow of
about fourscore and
four years, which departed
not from the temple, but
served God with fastings
and prayers night and day.

And she coming in that
instant gave thanks likewise
unto the Lord, and spake of
him to all them that looked
for redemption in Jerusalem.

And when they had performed
all things according to the
law of the Lord, they
returned into Galilee,
to their own city Nazareth.

And the child grew, and
waxed strong in spirit, filled
with wisdom: and the grace
of God was upon him.

Now his parents went
to Jerusalem every year at
the feast of the passover.

And when he was twelve years old,
they went up to Jerusalem after
the custom of the feast.

And when they had fulfilled
the days, as they returned,
the child Jesus tarried behind
in Jerusalem; and Joseph
and his mother knew not of it.

But they, supposing him to have
been in the company, went a day's
journey; and they sought him among
their kinsfolk and acquaintance.

And when they found him not,
they turned back again to
Jerusalem, seeking him.

And it came to pass,
that after three days they found
him in the temple, sitting in
the midst of the doctors,
both hearing them,
and asking them questions.

And all that heard him
were astonished at his
understanding
and answers.

And when they saw him, they were amazed: and his mother said unto him, Son, why hast thou thus dealt with us? behold, thy father and I have sought thee sorrowing.

And he said unto them,
How is it that ye sought me?
wist ye not that I must be
about my Father's business?

And they understood not the saying
which he spake unto them.

And he went down with them, and
came to Nazareth, and was subject
unto them: but his mother kept all
these sayings in her heart.

And Jesus increased in
wisdom and stature,
and in favour with
God and man.

CD PLAYLIST

Handel's Messiah

HIGHLIGHTS

PLAYING TIME: 75 min.

1. OVERTURE
2. RECIT.: COMFORT YE, MY PEOPLE, Jon Vickers, Tenor
3. AIR: EVERY VALLEY SHALL BE EXALTED, Jon Vickers, Tenor
4. CHORUS: AND HE SHALL PURIFY
5. AIR & CHORUS: O' THOU THAT TELLEST GOOD TIDINGS, Monica Sinclair, Mezzo-Soprano
6. CHORUS: FOR UNTO US A CHILD IS BORN
7. PASTORAL SYMPHONY
8. RECIT.: THERE WERE SHEPHERDS ABIDING, Jennifer Vyvyan, Soprano
9. RECIT.: AND THE ANGEL SAID UNTO THEM, Jennifer Vyvyan, Soprano
10. RECIT.: AND SUDDENLY THERE WAS . . . , Jennifer Vyvyan, Soprano
11. CHORUS: GLORY TO GOD IN THE HIGHEST
12. AIR: HE SHALL FEED HIS FLOCK; COME UNTO HIM, Monica Sinclair, Mezzo-Soprano, Jennifer Vyvyan, Soprano
13. CHORUS: SURELY HE HATH BORNE OUR GRIEFS
14. CHORUS: AND WITH HIS STRIPES WE ARE HEALED
15. CHORUS: ALL WE LIKE SHEEP HAVE GONE ASTRAY
16. CHORUS: HALLELUJAH!
17. AIR: I KNOW THAT MY REDEEMER LIVETH, Jennifer Vyvyan, Soprano
18. AIR: THE TRUMPET SHALL SOUND, Giorgio Tozzi, Bass
19. CHORUS: WORTHY IS THE LAMB